MW01006343

POINT YOUR
HEAD AND HEART...
YOUR ASS WILL FOLLOW

Think It...
Believe It...
Write It...
Move your Ass!

-CJ

Cover Photo by Breanne Cartright
Thanks to Kelli White for her help with the author bio

Published by Mindstir Media, LLC
45 Lafayette Rd | Suite 181| North Hampton, NH
03862 | USA
1.800.767.0531 | www.mindstirmedia.com

Printed in the United States of America
ISBN-13: 978-1-7341194-5-9

THE QJO INITIATIVE

POINT YOUR
HEAD AND HEART...
YOUR ASS WILL FOLLOW

AARON CHAPMAN, NJO

MINDSTIR MEDIA

EACH DAY THAT YOU ARE CONSCIOUS must include steps, regardless of how small, toward your greatest and best use; your individual purpose. Going a step further, one will notice over time consistent, conscious movement toward your purpose forces the subconscious to pave the path toward your destined end.

An individual's purpose needs to be defined. They need to find what is going to move their carcass every minute of every single day, what is it that is going to make them actually do something with their life rather than be constantly, aimlessly looking around at what will not be accomplished.

I had to come face to face with this question in an unexpected way. Joel Moyes, a very close friend of mine (damn near brother-ish) who owned a large real estate firm told me one evening while we were out with our wives that he was going change my life through an introduction to a lending company. He thought it would be a very good business move for me to connect with them. He had completed a deal that involved their two firms and was making it possible for me to potentially move my licenses to their organization. Walking different directions at our parting evening Joel yelled "I will change your life". The introduction led to my going through the application process and background checks.

After passing a background check, I was invited to the corporate office for an interview. Before they would schedule this interview, I was requested to complete a five-year vision exercise. I had never completed anything like this before. I was not a goal setter, vision caster, personal growth thinker, …. this exercise was quite foreign. As a way to help me understand the process, the CEO sent me his personal five-year exercise explaining what he intended to accomplish over a five-year window along with some general instruction. His particular write up contained a lot of bullet points in it. I understood what he was doing, where he was pointing himself, but I couldn't identify with a bullet point… I wanted something I could see, hear, feel. I wanted an experience. I chose to write in story format because bullet points didn't move me from my current state of familiar comfort.

I decided to write a letter to myself from a future time in my life. Five years in the future to be precise. Choosing to put myself in a setting along the famed Rubicon Trail. I was there with my wife Rizzo, sitting next to a fire, cooking steaks, thinking back about what I have accomplished over the previous five years. Describing the setting, sounds and the smells gave it a sense of reality to me.

The date came that I was to sit face to face with those who had charged me with this exercise. In our meeting I was singled out as submitting the most unique 5 year vision that they had seen. Because of this unique approach and my unique appearance, I was given some very encouraging feedback which gave me pause to really consider the depth of how this exercise can benefit my course in life.

Some of the old adages and regurgitated statements from those encouraging goal setting and envision ones future began to have some new meaning. The mere exercise of trying it brought about the sense of setting my bearing towards a distant result and checking it often, if not every day.

Deciding that this long-term exercise needed to be condensed to a more short-term exercise, I was determined to write down something similar for what I wanted to accomplish in 2017. February 4, 2017 I sat with a notepad and thoughtfully wrote the words to point toward what I was to accomplish before the end of that year that would contribute to the overall vision created years before in the five-year exercise. The last week of December 2016, I had closed on two Ozark mountain lots in northern Arkansas. This came about by constantly looking at this area online after stumbling across the little Arkansas town and just plain marveling at the beauty of the photos.

I had made mention on a call with a good friend, Lorne Shive in Memphis, that I had an interest in that particular town. In that mere statement he quickly hung up, called a contact and secured 5 lots (2 for me and 3 for him) right off Norfork Lake for an extremely low price. My back-of-the-mind focus on this area and allowing my focus to be known to the person with the right contacts yielded a result that I could not have completed on my own.

Since I had now owned property in the location that I had given thought to consistently for so long, I started a short-term vision set in the Ozark Mountain landscape on Feb 4th, 2017. Using the lesson that I was gifted in the five-year exercise, I created my short-term hybrid. It began with my sitting in a rocking chair on my porch looking out over the landscape of the northern Ozark Mountains. I described what I saw and heard, in detail. While sitting on that chair, I was looking back over the year 2017 and my accomplishments. I had set a goal of 600 transactions in January 2017, so I used that goal as part of my list of completed items in this vision.

In addition to writing this down, I decided to incorporate daily disciplines. Humans are creatures of habit. All mankind become slaves to the habits they have formed over the years. I made the conscious decision to become a slave to good habits. I hated reading, writing, hell…thinking was a task I shrunk from. Concentration for any length of time was very hard!

I discovered many who have already done the researching, vetting and deep thinking on innumerable subjects. If I were to form good habits, I would incorporate the study of much of their effort. I began with the writings of Napoleon Hill. I devoured his writings and re-read, "Think and Grow Rich, Outwitting the Devil and Wisdom of Success" three times each. The message was impossible to ignore. In short order, my grasp of the points I had learned were to be tested.

Not long after writing my vision I had my resolve tested. I received a call from my Regional Manager asking how important the state of Missouri was to my business. Looking up the stats, it appeared to be 12% of my volume. This made it a pretty important state for my business. When I inquired as to why I was being asked, the reply explained that the company's license, as well as my license, was being put on inactive status because we were losing our brick and mortar (physical location) in that state because the only licensed resident was resigning.

At closer examination, I saw that I had in excess of thirty transactions pending in Missouri. "What is the plan?", I inquired. Ads on Facebook, Craigslist and job sites was what was presented to me. That was not acceptable. I felt a need to jump in there and make something happen myself. I asked if I had latitude to "solve the problem myself". When given the confirmation that I could do this, I called my sister who lived in Missouri.

Feeling significant pressure at this point, I made the call to Breanne, my younger sister, the moment I hung up from the previous call. When she answered, I immediately asked ,"Hey Breezor (nickname from childhood), you wanna get licensed?". "I haven't heard from you in six months and this is the first thing you say to me...You wanna get licensed?" She replied. "Yup", I confirmed. I then heard a crack in her voice as she began to tell me that this was an answer to prayer. She and her husband Jim had literally discussed the very same thing the day before. She had been cleaning vacation rentals for some time. The owner recently sold them, leaving her without a job. Jim does well with his job, but the cost of living was just pushing the limits of his income. They needed something else.

Since she had worked with me years before Jim suggested "Why don't you call your brother and see if he has any spots open"

After hearing her story, "Is that a Yes?" was my reply. Again I was under pressure and had to solve a problem. Her loud "Of course that is a YES!" was all I wanted to hear. I wasn't paying attention to her motivation like I should have. I didn't grasp the forces at work in the background. No matter...I was about to very shortly. After our conversation, all the necessary steps were put in motion. She was provided the education materials and began her required licensing education hours in preparation to test. Additionally we prepared all the necessary information to license her home, as that is what was done for the previous licensed resident. All was in motion and my grace period on my license was coming to an end. The Missouri files in process unfortunately were not going to get done in the grace period, so I really needed Breanne's license to get completed. The weekend before her test came and I had multiple anxious callers checking in on our status. "She is testing Monday" I would reply and encourage them that we were ready to roll as soon as her license came through. She was well prepared and was doing extremely well on her practice tests. There was no reason to fret.

Monday came and I anxiously awaited her good news. Finally my phone rang with her caller ID notifying me of her call. I picked up with excitement to hear what appeared to be sobbing coming from the caller. "I am so sorry....I missed it by one question" is what came to me through the phone. My heart sank....I was overcome with a cloud of impossibility. "Please tell me you're kidding" I pleaded, as I did not want to face this. I had folks in Kansas City and St Louis under a ton of pressure and we needed this to go through.

I had put all my eggs in that basket. She couldn't test for another 30 days and by that time, we would lose all these transactions. Another thought flashed in my head. I calmed her down and said, "All will be ok, I got it covered". "How?" she asked. "I am booking flights and I will be there Thursday. Please find every commercial location I can rent and everything I can buy." "Why is that?" she asked. "I am moving to Missouri", I replied.

I had twenty-three licenses and if I was the licensed person in the state with commercial office space I could transfer my licenses, then I would be able to get the thing fired back up. It should be really simple. I checked with my licensing department. They believed that would work, so we put the plan in motion.

Landing in Missouri with my wife, Rizzo, and son, Derek, we rented a car and went straight to Breanne's house. She invited us in to see the kids and relax from our trip. "Nope…Get your ass in the car, we are gonna look at the properties you found" were my first words to her. I was on a mission. Touring the potential spaces, there was one solid possibility. A little single office that I could rent at a Senior's Center owned by the city of Branson. It would fill all the needs, but we had to wait for the current tenant to be out.

While thinking about that one and the others, we looked at, Breanne pointed us to a place Jim thought I would like to see. We rolled up on two older frontier-style cabins covered in vegetation and somewhat run down. We called the number on the sign and waited for the agent to come open them up for us. Walking through them, Rizzo and I looked at each other and decided on the spot.

We were going to buy them. The negotiations started immediately.

There was no way to finance these in any traditional manner. They were not at all functional in their current state. In addition, they sat on seven acres of Ozark Mountain property. The land-value to improvement ratio would make it really tough to finance even if it were functional. The seller would have to agree to a carry the note to have any shot at not having to pay cash for the whole thing.

We reached an agreement while we were there that week and prepared to close within two weeks. Once closing had finished, I scheduled time to meet a contractor on site which I would need to travel back to Missouri to do. Tickets were purchased and another trip was underway. I rented another vehicle in Springfield and drove back down to Branson. When I stepped out if the vehicle onto the deck, I looked over to the porch of the cabin that was to be the office and there sat a rocking chair. The words that escaped my lips were "Shit yeah! I have a rocking chair!"

Taking large strides, I stepped up on the porch, sat down in the chair, and began to rock back and forth and look at the landscape of my new purchase. An immediate rush of realization forced the involuntary formation of goosebumps. I was sitting on my porch, in my rocking chair, overlooking the Ozark Mountain Landscape. Two months and two days prior, I described this scene in my notepad envisioning accomplishments for 2017.

My revelry was broken by the sound of my sister pulling up in her minivan with her head out the window screaming "You weren't supposed to see that yet". "How did this get here?" I hollered back. She walked down the railroad tie steps toward me and said "Rizzo called me and insisted that a rocking chair be waiting for you on the porch when you get here. Jim knew a guy who hand made them and he talked him out of the first one he ever made".

Declaring my vision in writing and sharing that vision with one who was most important to me, fulfilled the realization of it. I may not have thought to place that chair there, but the collaborative effort of my closest friend, my Rizzo, and my little sis, brought about the materialization of my mental picture. I learned another important lesson about sharing a thought or goal with others whom you care for and trust. What detail may be overlooked by us can be put in place by another. If shared with one who has malicious intent toward you this oversight can be magnified and used in a way to derail your efforts. Choose wisely those who you trust with your future.

Returning home I put all my energy into the transfer. I submitted all my paperwork to the licensing department. After several days of documentation changing hands, the department manager contacted me indicating several state licensing departments said that I could not transfer my license, I have to re-apply, and it could take thirty days. DAMMIT, here I was back at the thirty day wait thing AGAIN!!!

I did not have thirty days. No matter how much energy I put forth or resources I exhausted, the elements demanded thirty days! Since Breezor did not pass the first test, she had to wait thirty days to retake it. I looked at the days that had passed and found she could retake it in two weeks. At this point, I called her back up and told her she was going to retake the exam on the first day that is available since my plan B would not work.

I could feel the anxiety build on the other side of the phone. She had become so reliant on my plan B that she had not continued to study materials and backed off of the idea that she could retest anytime soon. It really boiled down to her being very self-conscious about this and doubtful that she would be able to pass. I tried to encourage her, but it was evident her internal thinking was blocking her from making this work, so I had her restart her studies and I booked myself another flight.

As the days passed in preparation for my flight, I received the bid from the contractor. The sorry sumbitch didn't give me a heads up to be sitting when he sent it. The bottom line figure was an "estimate" which he made sure to point out did not include labor or his 15%. He may as well run me over with a loaded dump truck and then honked the horn after, flattening me to the pavement. My trip would allow me to kill two birds with one stone. Sit with my sister to help her prepare for her test and secure another contractor. There was no way I was gonna proceed with what I was given by the contractor nor would I accept the circumstances associated with my licenses. I had other plans and by damn, I would execute on them!

Breanne, Jim, and I went to dinner when I got into Branson. I encouraged Breanne to tell me all about her fears associated with the test. I then handed her a note pad and a pen and explained to her that I needed her to think in great detail what it would be like to pass the test. She needed to write down this experience starting with her sitting in front of the computer at the testing center staring at the pop-up screen at the end of the test that has a button to click labeled "Are you finished....Yes/ No".

After a few minutes of thought and some interactive spit-balling, Breanne placed the tip of the pen on the paper and started dragging the ink out into script. In her concentration, she began to feel the emotion of the event she was creating. Not many lines into it there was a look of peace to her appearance. Tears began to swell in her eyes as she was pouring her whole soul into this page. Three pages later she paused, stared at her emotions placed in ink, and placed the pen down on the table.

She slid the papers over to me for my review. Reading through them, I could put myself in her chair at the test center and feel the anxiety pulsing through her as she paused before clicking "Yes". As I read, I could feel what she was feeling, and experience the whole event as if it was me taking the test. When I finished my read, I began formulating my vision of where I am during the time she is taking her test and awaiting her call. I was detailing out my response when I answer the phone to hear her voice cracking on the other end of the call with news of triumph over what had deflated her just weeks before. Handing her my two pages, I passed her vision over to Jim and suggested he do as I did. My instructions to Breanne were to dig in and study her ass off. When she feels that twinge of doubt or fear creep in she needed to pull out these pages and read them. Feel the emotion of her experience passing the test which was already set in motion. She also needed to read the reinforcement of the experience written by Jim and me. Each time she did this it would set her back on course with her mind and heart pointed to the successful end her ass had no choice but to follow.

The appointed day of the re-test arrived and I too found myself pulling out the written words of Breanne's successful experience at the testing center. I needed the positive influence of its message as much as she did at that point. I was not going to allow doubt or fear to creep in and put to work universal forces to hedge up her way toward her determined goal. We spoke several times leading up to the final hour. Only positive communication was had. She confirmed her constant reading of the vision and confidently went into her appointment.

What felt like a week passed and her number finally appeared on my caller ID as her call was coming in. As the words of her vision foretold, Breanne's excited and decidedly relieved tones came through the speaker declaring that she had successfully completed the test. Relief swept through me starting with the ear that heard the news and permeated my entire being. This news allowed me to move toward the next step in the process; getting the location licensed so we could continue business. Calls were made to all who were awaiting this news with a detail on the next steps that needed to take place to activate the licenses again and fulfill my obligation to them and their business.

This was a very tough experience. The mental effort required was not a small labor. However, it cemented my knowledge of the fact the that the power within us is there and on tap at any time we chose to use it. It is not in just being able to accomplish, but greater power is the resetting of any sort of doubt we might have. The moment-by-moment battle we face in anxious thought can be defeating. Feeling strong and capable through consistent evaluation of where your heading and personal reinforcement separates those who successfully do and those who successfully don't.

Helping yourself stay on your path through constant heading checks is an absolute necessity. The instant we allow ourselves to look from our path or become a victim of untargeted busyness, there is an increased chance that we can be drawn into an activity that does not fulfill our purpose. Giving our attention to any other activity that does not contribute to achieving our vision, results in complete derailment. Albeit, very subtle changes in our focus each day with very small movement away can yield catastrophic results. Have you ever seen a derailed train? The tracks are very thin and only inches off their set path can create a huge catastrophe. How much effort is required to put a train back on its tracks?

If you are going to focus on something, why not focus on your biggest goal? Why not put the limited energy you are going to have every day towards that? You are going to be active and engaged in something. The question: Is the energy you are expending contributing to that or is it taking away from it? The only way to ensure proper direction is to evaluate what it is that you are doing and how it is contributing to your great end every single day.

When I wrote my vision, I was looking more toward my goal of closing 600 units in 2017 more so than the setting I decided to write about. I had no need to go to Missouri, I had no need to go and buy anything in the Ozarks at that time, but because I wrote it down, by circumstance and my will to bend circumstance to meet my needs, I was able to accomplish my goal with success. I closed 676 transactions in 2017 and as a result of a shared vision, more was accomplished. The loan originator in St. Louis who quit, the corporate folks who accepted my desire to solve the problem myself, Breanne's need to test a second time, an unrelenting team pushing past 600 units amidst increasing pressures, and my Rizzo.

You do not have the luxury of wandering aimlessly through existence. You are serving no purpose drifting with the current of circumstance. All circumstance is an effect. Your focus and chosen thought is the cause. If you do not like the effect...Correct the cause. Write it down and share it with your Rizzo!

CPSIA information can be obtained
at www.ICGtesting.com
Printed in the USA
JSHW010528160520
5718JS00006B/93

9 781734 119459

On Saturday afternoon
Betsy Bear visits the local craft show.

At the potter's stall,
Betsy watches the potter turn the wheel.

She shapes the clay with her hands
and forms it into a round, fat jug.

She paints the dried clay with a glaze
and puts it in the kiln to be fired.

Betsy Bear sees the finished pots, each one different and lovely. She gives thanks for the skill and care of the potter.

At the weaver's stall, Betsy watches
the weaver making the cloth.

He chooses the threads from the shelf
and admires the colours.

He sets up the loom and passes
the shuttle backwards and forwards.

Betsy Bear feels the bright cloth,
strong and warm. She gives thanks for
the skill and care of the weaver.

At the woodcarver's stall, Betsy watches
the carver chiselling the wood.

He handles the wood with care
and carves it into a new shape.

He rubs down the wood with beeswax
and polishes it until it shines.

Betsy Bear sees the wooden shapes,
round and gleaming. She gives thanks
for the skill and care of the carver.

At the jewellery stall, Betsy watches
the jeweller making a fine necklace.

She sorts the delicate beads
and tries them in different patterns.

She threads each bead onto the fine thread and ties a knot to hold it in place.

Betsy Bear handles the pretty necklaces, smooth and sparkling. She gives thanks for the skill and care of the jeweller.

On Sunday afternoon
Betsy Bear visits the country park.

She hears the birds on the rooftop,
so tuneful and clear.

She smells the plants and grasses,
so fragrant and sweet.

She touches the bark of the trees,
so rough and strong.

Betsy Bear sees the changing pattern of the sky, so delicate and fine. She gives thanks for the skill and care of God the Creator.

In *The Craft Show*, Betsy Bear's experience of the skill and care of the potter, weaver, woodcarver and jeweller helps her to enter into Jeremiah's experience at the potter's house in Jeremiah 18:

> 'The Lord said to me, "Go down to the potter's house, where I will give you my message". So I went there and saw the potter working at his wheel. Whenever a piece of pottery turned out imperfect, he would take the clay and make it into something else. Then the Lord said to me, "Haven't I the right to do with you people of Israel what the potter did with the clay? You are in my hands just like the clay in the potter's hands."'

The following questions suggest further ways of developing the links between the young child's experience, the story and the Bible passage.

Talk about different kinds of craft:

What craft activities do you enjoy?

Why do you enjoy them?

What kind of things do you like to make?

How do you feel when you have made something new?

Do members of your family have craft hobbies?

What do they make?

Take a look around your house.

What objects can you find which have been made by skilled craftspeople?

How many different colours, shapes and textures can you find?

Talk about the story:

What stalls did Betsy Bear visit at the craft show?

What did she see?

What did she touch?

What did she smell?

What did Betsy Bear see at the country park?

What did she hear?

What did she touch?

What did she smell?

Think some more about the story:

What other stalls might Betsy Bear have visited at the craft show?

What other objects might she have seen?

What sounds might she have heard?

What smells might she have smelt?

What other things might she have seen, heard or touched at the country park?

Think about the Bible passage:

Imagine you are visiting the potter's house with Jeremiah.

What do you see?

What do you hear?

What do you smell?

What is the potter making?

What do you learn about the skill and care of God the Creator?

Titles in the Teddy Horsley series:

Teddy Horsley Big Books:
LARGE format books with LARGE words and pictures, designed for Key Stage 1 and Pre-school. Perfect for reading to groups of children; suitable for RE and Literacy Hour.

Teddy Horsley Activity Pack:
- ❖ One *Teddy Horsley* book
- ❖ *Teddy Horsley* activity book
- ❖ *Teddy Horsley* picture card
- ❖ *Teddy Horsley* cotton tidybag
- ❖ Crayons
- ❖ Removable stickers